What Are Your Large Fries and Soda?

The Tale

Welcome to a marketing tale. This story begins like all the others:

Once upon a time, there was a small and picturesque restaurant that offered, among other things, "all-beef" burgers, "tempting" cheeseburgers, "Golden" French fries, milkshakes, sodas, and milk. The protagonist of this story will be called "McDaniels" and he was responsible for feeding and entertaining the cheerful inhabitants of the kingdom of San Bernardino (if I had to guess, it would be in California, USA).

McDaniels began to succeed thanks to his delicious dishes, affordable prices, and a creative combination of communication and customer experience that made people feel proud and happy to visit, not just for the food but for the pleasant experience.

Over time, McDaniels couldn't keep up with the demand, and many potential customers left due to long wait times. One of the owners wondered: "What if we could devise a more efficient method of preparing food? After all, our menu isn't that complex," and they set to work.

After several ideas, discussions, and trials, they came up with a real-time production line system, allowing them to serve more customers in less time, reducing the cost per product and increasing both their revenue and profits. McDaniels was a promising and growing business.

With the arrival of a "strange enemy" disguised as a wolf to gain the owners' trust, a chain of restaurants was created with the famous name, growing indiscriminately throughout the United States and achieving incredible sales. It's worth mentioning that part of the business was in real estate, but we'll leave that tale for another time.

As the chain grew and adopted the franchise model, it is credited with creating the concept of "Fast Food." Today, we associate that term with junk food, but when it was created, it literally meant food (nourishment for body and soul) that was fast (faster than hunger could make you angry).

Seeing McDaniels' success, the villains of the story appeared. We'll call them "Copycats," including Burger Evil, Prince Bad, Up-N-Down Burger, John in the Bag, and Whotheburger, among others.

With such strong competition accumulating over 20 villainous chains, they all began fighting for the kingdoms with the largest populations, leading to a price war. A price war wasn't what McDaniels had in mind, but there was nothing they could do.

McDaniels' war squad traveled until they found the Fairy of Profitability to seek advice and received a well-intentioned but business-ignorant mandate: "You must compete on price, reduce the quality of your products, and be faster than anyone else." Thus, the situation that today makes us associate them with the term "Junk Food" began.

The war grew and grew (it didn't blow and blow) to the point where several villains died of starvation, unable to compete with the aggressive prices their rivals and their fairy godmothers placed on the products. It reached such a low point that they began using black magic called "Marketing," naming the products, arranging the points of sale, and building large signs taller than any castle towers.

This magic worked for a while, but prices remained low, which was inevitable. No power could get the villains and McDaniels to work together to stabilize those costs.

They reached a point of no return: either choose a strategy to improve profitability or die from the sin of overreach. And so, combos were created.

McDaniels understood that only a small fraction of their customers bought a package, for example, a burger, fries, and soda. It was known that selling fries and sodas was more profitable than selling burgers, but they couldn't stop selling the main product.

The combo sold all three products at a lower price than the sum of these on the menu, but still, the marginality increased. They went from selling 2 fries and 5 sodas for every 10 burgers to selling 7 fries and 7 sodas for every 10 burgers. McDaniels had saved the day, but greed (another sin) took over—they wanted more!

This is where "sizes" were "invented."

Well, sizes have always existed, and although they say size doesn't matter, in this tale, it does.

So, you could buy a single-patty burger or small fries or a tiny soda for fewer silver coins. But you could also buy a triple-patty burger accompanied by large fries and soda, of course, paying a few more coins.

Gradually, McDaniels' business model changed. Burgers, the main product, would cover fixed and variable costs. These costs included the supplies and disposables for fries and sodas, so each additional order of fries and sodas was 100% profit for the business. Combo prices approached very small levels; the burger would be the same, but the complement sizes would change with minimal perceived price.

In this way, burgers continued to contribute significantly to the business's maintenance, and combos increased revenue and profitability. As the differences between packages were so small, with significantly lower complement costs also covered by selling the main product, the business's goal became selling as many combos and/or large-size complements as possible.

This strategic adjustment is the reason why today (and after almost 100 years) we can enjoy their delicious products (increasingly less delicious) in considerably larger sizes (not really that much) at very affordable prices (not that affordable today).

The villain competitors have copied the model to a greater or lesser extent. Thus, the price and strategy war, where this tale of disaster began, has resumed. However, now they compete with models that manage to be profitable thanks to the high-margin complements.

But the tale doesn't end there. In the kingdom of San Bernardino, McDaniels decided to keep innovating. They realized that not only the products but also the customer experience could be a source of revenue. They began redesigning their restaurants, creating more welcoming and attractive environments with play areas for children and free WiFi (a strange futuristic signal) for adults. These improvements increased customers' dwell time, which in turn increased consumption.

Moreover, McDaniels introduced a mobile app that allowed customers to place orders and pay from their phones. This innovation not only improved efficiency but also provided McDaniels with a gold mine of data on customer preferences. They used this data to personalize offers and promotions, further increasing customer loyalty and sales.

McDaniels' strategy also included expanding the menu to include healthier options, responding to a growing demand from health-conscious consumers. They offered salads, fruits, and low-calorie options, which attracted a new segment of customers who previously avoided fast food. Although these options were not as profitable as fries and sodas, they improved the brand's perception as a place that cares about its customers' well-being.

This combination of customer experience improvements, technological innovation, and menu diversification allowed McDaniels to stay relevant and competitive in a saturated market. The lesson is clear: adaptation and evolution are essential for long-term success.

What seems like a small offer is actually a brilliant tactic to increase profitability. Those few extra cents per customer quickly add up, and at the end of the day, they represent a significant portion of the establishment's profits.

And so, McDaniels' business model became a benchmark. Their strategy of selling low-cost, high-margin complements proved extremely effective. Although the price war remains a constant battle, the key to success lies in the ability to adapt and evolve strategies to stay competitive and profitable. This is something any business can learn and implement in their own context.

McDaniels not only survived the price war but thrived by focusing on what really mattered: customer satisfaction and sustainable profitability. By identifying and exploiting their "large fries and sodas," they found a winning formula that allowed them to not only survive but also lead in an extremely competitive market.

All of this leaves us with the lesson of why today, every time we go to a place like this, we are always disciplined and passionate enough to be asked: "Would you like to upgrade to large fries and soda for just 1 more dollar?"

This is just a tale. Any resemblance to reality is NOT purely coincidental. Characters have been created and parts of the story adjusted for ultra-dramatic purposes.

Pablo Talks

This part of each story I will tell is merely an opinion. It is a space I created to express myself. Each story you read will be based on a truth, and each section following "Pablo Talks" will be a concise, quantitative, and compelling analysis so you can apply the strategies of others in your work, your business, your ventures, and your ability to innovate and create solutions based on proven successful facts. But Pablo Talks... is just an opinion.

I could say that I think McDaniels is a story of success in the face of adversity, but no. There are other stories for that, but mainly because this is not an adversity as such. It is a continuity present in the day-to-day operations of all businesses; it is an operational issue, because we cannot control the competition, but we can control how we tactically react to it.

I have seen through more than 500 clients I have had the fortune to serve how the fear of facing competitive markets and creating solutions based on demand, finance, and creativity prevents them from being bold and trying new ways to operate the business they already know, and they prefer to wait until the water reaches too high to react.

For me, this story is initially about survival, but in its later stages, it's about maximizing profitability strategies. It is true that the mentioned chains do not change "from teeth outwards"; they remain fast food chains selling burgers and offering an experience through very precise and specific marketing executions. But when options ran out, they didn't have much choice and made substantial decisions from a financial profile: "Let's put profitability and profits where it doesn't seem like they are."

I would love for you to get some interesting ideas from this story to apply wherever you want and thus maximize your profits. A very important point I want to touch on is that you don't have to be on the edge; the water doesn't have to be up to your neck. You can continue to be highly profitable and use this tactic as an addition to your catalog, thereby increasing your turnover, profits, profitability, and growth. What I mean is that if we learn the story properly, the smartest thing is not to repeat what went wrong but to apply what went right.

When the idea of "Tales of Marketing" came to me, I discussed it with a good friend. He is in real estate; he is a broker. I told him about my project to write "Stories with commercial applications" and also told him specifically about this one. He said he thought the idea was good but that I should be careful not to leave out very large segments. Some of his words were: "Surely that worked for McDaniels and might work for other restaurants or consumer products, but for me, it's impossible to apply."

His words resonated and left me thinking for several minutes (and later for several days), but at the moment I said, "Help me prove that's not true; let's think of a way to apply this methodology to help you." There was incredulity; he expressed the fact that he only sold houses. What else could he do?

A week later, he called me and said, "I have it." I don't want to overexpose his strategy, but we met to plan and innovate, and broadly speaking, what he did was contact a medium-sized construction company to create synergy. When offering the houses, he always found one or two areas for improvement that were neither very complicated nor very expensive. He offered potential clients to repair that specific section if they bought the houses (addition of services) at a very attractive price. At the same time, he asked the sellers for their approval so that in case of selling the house, they would bear a small additional cost for that repair.

In short, if his commission was $10,000 USD, he offered a repair worth $5,000 USD at a price of $1,500 USD for the home buyer. He would charge the sellers an additional $2,500 USD on top of the commission to fulfill the promise that made the sale possible, and he would contribute $1,000 USD from his earnings. This achieved several things, although at first, it did not seem to favor his profitability.

Now, the sales efforts were less. He used to show each house an average of 10 to 15 times, and that decreased to 5-8 times. This is a significant improvement in profitability by time. Additionally, by partnering with a proven quality company, in several cases, he ended up doing additional work (which is not his "Core Business"), now with full prices and profit for him.

In addition to that benefit, he had more properties on offer, and at the same time, more clients wanted to buy from him by getting the benefit of the improvement. And having an improvement in temporal profitability, he was able to manage many more properties much more efficiently and effectively.

What seemed impossible in an initial conversation turned into a great change for him. From selling between 15 and 20 properties a year, today he sells almost 50, and has 5 people supporting him internally. Additionally, he always has improvement work on the properties, which does not take time but brings him profits. And the associated company has been loyal to him because the next job would only come through his sales.

His profits increased by a total of 250% in 2 years. I am talking about money that goes into his account, an undeniable reality, and it all started with a conversation about this story. It also helped me decide to write these stories.

With this, I want to emphasize 2 points:

1.   It doesn't have to be an easy or logical idea. It is most likely that it will take you time and effort to even come up with a concept, but it seems worth it.

2.   If a fast-food chain strategy could be "transferred" to real estate, it can be transferred to practically any business or industry.

The following chapters will have similar stories. But the stories, strategies, and applications will be different. If with these 12 stories I can get readers to apply 3 or 4 strategies to their businesses, I will be achieving the goal of "Marketing Tales."

Next, you will be able to read:

•   A numerical profitability exercise from the McDaniels story

•   An example of how someone has already done it in a different industry

•   The 10 relevant and breaking points extracted from the McDaniels story

•   The 10 steps to follow to execute the strategy in your business (that is, a step-by-step guide for you to do it yourself)

•   And a short conclusion.

If you only bought the E-Book of **What are your large fries and soda?** and you liked it, I would love for you to give the full book a chance. It is called **Marketing Tales: The Inexplicable Application of Commercial Strategies from One Business to Another**. It will be available soon!

I have had a wonderful experience writing this. I have informed and educated myself in many stories and commercial and marketing strategies. I believe the goal of reaching people can be achieved, but from the outset, it has already served me a lot.

Thank you for your time in reading this, and I leave you with the next section of McDaniels, a simple and illustrative financial exercise.

The Exercise

WARNING: If you're not interested in applying this strategy right now and you're not a fan of numbers, skip this section. It's informative but boring.

Let's use illustrative applications (though closely aligned with real percentages) to understand how these strategies behave.

Initial Strategy

Direct menu strategy, traditional operation, one location:

- Fixed Costs: $100 USD
- Variable Costs: 33%
- Price of a burger: $5 USD
- Burger profitability: 40%
- Contribution per burger: $2
- Price of fries: $2 USD
- Fries profitability: 80%
- Contribution per fries: $1.6
- Price of a soda: $1.5 USD
- Soda profitability: 80%
- Contribution per soda: $1.2
- Sales distribution: Burgers 59% / Fries 12% / Sodas 29%

- Break-even point: 59 sales (35 burgers / 7 fries / 17 sodas)

- Profitability at 100 sales: $72

- Profitability at 500 sales: $760

- Profitability at 810 sales: $1,293.2

Production Line Strategy

When the production line formula was found, the variable cost indicator in the profitability formula was affected. Additionally, sales increased by meeting total demand:

- Fixed Costs: $100 USD

- Variable Costs: 27%

- Price of a burger: $5 USD

- Burger profitability: 50%

- Contribution per burger: $2.5

- Price of fries: $2 USD

- Fries profitability: 88%

- Contribution per fries: $1.76

- Price of a soda: $1.5 USD

- Soda profitability: 80%

- Contribution per soda: $1.2

- Sales distribution: Burgers 59% / Fries 12% / Sodas 29%

- Break-even point: 49 sales (29 burgers / 6 fries / 14 sodas)

- Profitability at 100 sales: $103.42

- Profitability at 500 sales: $917.1

- Profitability at 1,120 sales: $2,178.3

- Change in profits: +65%

Chain Expansion Strategy

With chain expansion, fixed costs increased due to the pursuit of high commercial value properties, but sales also increased with greater brand awareness and the perfection of the production line:

- Fixed Costs: $133 USD

- Variable Costs: 27%

- Price of a burger: $5 USD

- Burger profitability: 50%

- Contribution per burger: $2.5

- Price of fries: $2 USD

- Fries profitability: 88%

- Contribution per fries: $1.76

- Price of a soda: $1.5 USD

- Soda profitability: 80%

- Contribution per soda: $1.2

- Sales distribution: Burgers 59% / Fries 12% / Sodas 29%

- Break-even point: 66 sales (39 burgers / 8 fries / 19 sodas)

- Profitability at 100 sales: $70.42

- Profitability at 500 sales: $884.4

- Profitability at 1,450 sales: $2,616.59

- Change in profits: +29%

Saturated Market Strategy

In a saturated market, fixed and variable costs, as well as sales distribution, remained the same. However, a price war began and sales suffered a bit. Moreover, profits now had to be shared between the franchise owner and the brand owner:

- Fixed Costs: $133 USD

- Variable Costs: 27%

- Price of a burger: $3.5 USD

- Burger profitability: 50%

- Contribution per burger: $1.75

- Price of fries: $1.5 USD

- Fries profitability: 88%

- Contribution per fries: $1.32

- Price of a soda: $1.3 USD

- Soda profitability: 80%

- Contribution per soda: $1.04

- Sales distribution: Burgers 59% / Fries 12% / Sodas 29%

- Break-even point: 90 sales (53 burgers / 11 fries / 26 sodas)

- Profitability at 100 sales: $16.25

- Profitability at 500 sales: $613.25

- Profitability at 980 sales: $1,329.65

- Change in profits: -53%

Combo Strategy

By adjusting the strategy to combos, the sale of fries and sodas, which have higher profitability, increased, although their prorated price in the package dropped a bit. Sales spiked with the combos. The sales goal increased, but since combos are 3 sales in 1 person, it wasn't a problem:

- Fixed Costs: $133 USD

- Variable Costs: 27%

- Price of a burger: $3.5 USD

- Burger profitability: 50%

- Contribution per burger: $1.75

- Price of fries: $1.28 USD

- Fries profitability: 88%

- Contribution per fries: $1.12

- Price of a soda: $1.11 USD

- Soda profitability: 80%

- Contribution per soda: $0.88

- Sales distribution: Burgers 42% / Fries 29% / Sodas 29%

- Break-even point: 94 sales (39 burgers / 27 fries / 27 sodas)

- Profitability at 100 sales: $8.94

- Profitability at 500 sales: $576.7

- Profitability at 2,460 sales: $3,358.72

- Change in profits: +152%

Master Strategy

The master strategy consisted of reducing the size of the fries and sodas in the combos without changing the menu cost or the absorption in the prorate. The fixed and variable costs would be entirely charged to the burger, and all additional sales would be 100% profitable. Combo sales increased, generating automatic profitability, and with the "Upgrade" of the combo to medium or large, without moving costs, profits maximized. All this while respecting the price war!

The calculation of sales and the way profitability was calculated had to be reconfigured, resulting in something like this (individual complement sales are calculated as zero since with combos it doesn't make sense):

- Fixed Costs: $133 USD

- Variable Costs: 30%

- Price of a burger: $3.5 USD with a contribution of $0.35

- Price of Combo 1: $5.5 USD with a contribution of $2.35

- Price of Combo 2: $6 USD with a contribution of $2.85

- Price of Combo 3: $6.5 USD with a contribution of $3.35

- Sales distribution: Burgers 6% / Combo Small 17% / Combo Medium 33% / Combo Large 44%

- Break-even point: 47 sales (3 burgers / 8 small combos / 15 medium combos / 21 large combos)

- Profitability at 100 sales: $154.20

- Profitability at 500 sales: $1,328.7

- Profitability at 2,460 sales: $7,083.26

- Change in profits: +110%

- Change in profits from the initial business model: +447%

Summary Table

Strategy	Fixed Costs (USD)	Var Costs (%)	Sales Distribution	Break Even	Base sales profitability (USD)	Profit Change (%)
Initial	100	33	H. 59% / P. 12% / S. 29%	59 ventas (35H / 7P / 17S)	1,293.2	-
Line Production	100	27	H. 59% / P. 12% / S. 29%	49 ventas (29H / 6P / 14S)	2,178.3	+65%
Chain Expansion	133	27	H. 59% / P. 12% / S. 29%	66 ventas (39H / 8P / 19S)	2,616.59	+29%
Saturated Market	133	27	H. 59% / P. 12% / S. 29%	90 ventas (53H / 11P / 26S)	1,329.65	-53%
Combo Strategy	133	27	H. 42% / P. 29% / S 29%	94 ventas (39H / 27P / 27S)	3,358.72	+152%
Master Strategy	133	30	H. 6% / C Ch 17% / C M 33% / C G 44%	47 ventas (3H / 8Ch / 15M / 21G)	7,083.26	+110%
Total Change						+447%

The Example

I will give an example of a company dedicated to selling assemble-it-yourself furniture. Its business model has been innovative, producing furniture online and selling it in boxes much smaller than the furniture itself, revolutionizing the market first in Europe and then in America in an aggressive and very profitable manner. Let's call it "OK.EA."

OK.EA, a revolutionary force in the home industry, has defied conventions since its inception in Sweden in 1943. Known as much more than a simple furniture store, OK.EA, whose name evokes the essence of its mission and vision, has earned a privileged place in the hearts of millions of people around the world. Through a visionary strategy, OK.EA has demonstrated that the true potential of profitability lies not so much in the main products but in the complementary ones.

What began as a modest furniture store on the outskirts of Stockholm has flourished into a global home empire. OK.EA has remained steadfast in its commitment to making quality design accessible to everyone, but its success lies in its expansion into a wide range of complementary products and services.

OK.EA has unraveled the secret of profitability by understanding that complementary products possess a much greater financial potential than the main products. As customers walk through OK.EA's vast stores, they not only find main furniture items but also a plethora of home products that complement and enrich the shopping experience.

From kitchen utensils to decorative textiles, OK.EA offers a complete range of products that not only meet customers' needs but also significantly increase the company's revenue. These complementary products have proven to be an invaluable source of profitability, transforming the traditional perception of where true value lies in the home industry.

OK.EA has redefined the shopping experience by turning it into a journey of inspiration and discovery. OK.EA stores are not mere points of sale; they are design sanctuaries where customers can immerse themselves in different styles of decor and smart home solutions.

But the OK.EA experience doesn't stop at physical stores. The company has integrated innovative technology, such as augmented reality apps and interior design software, to allow customers to visualize how products would look in their own space. This fusion of the physical and digital creates a personalized and immersive shopping experience that increases customer loyalty and, consequently, the company's profitability.

In addition to its impressive range of products, OK.EA offers a series of services that add value and convenience for customers. From kitchen and closet planning services to home delivery and assembly, OK.EA strives to make the shopping experience as smooth and seamless as possible.

These services not only increase customer satisfaction but also generate additional revenue for the company. OK.EA has shown that the key to sustainable profitability lies in offering not only quality products but also services that enhance the overall customer experience.

OK.EA is committed not only to improving the lives of its customers but also to protecting the planet and supporting disadvantaged communities around the world. The company has implemented a series of initiatives to reduce its environmental impact, such as the use of sustainable materials and supply chain optimization.

Moreover, OK.EA has invested in community development and economic empowerment programs in developing countries, demonstrating its commitment to corporate social responsibility. These actions not only generate a positive impact in the world but also strengthen the company's long-term reputation and profitability.

In summary, OK.EA has redefined the home industry landscape by demonstrating that true profitability lies in complementary products. From its innovative approach to the customer experience to its commitment to sustainability and social responsibility, OK.EA continues to be an undisputed leader in its field. With a bold vision and impeccable execution, OK.EA has shown that true business success goes beyond numbers; it's about transforming lives and homes around the world.

The 10 Turning Points

This section seems important because it helps us gain a greater context of the case without having to bear the weight of the story in details such as prices or the complementary product strategy.

The story of a company is composed of multiple situations that we must consider, and we should not forget that the tale, opinion, and example are simply a commercial strategy, which, although it was key, was not everything.

The 10 points accompany the same story, they do not forget what we have read so far, but they help us generate more context and have a better understanding of the situation. To avoid making the reading longer, here are the 10 points:

1. Innovation in Production:

I always like to start with the part where the winning concept is conceived, that differentiator that eventually becomes the decision that led them to true success. For me, this is the first key point in almost any success story. I like to think that entrepreneurs and founders look back a few years and think, "Wow, that made the difference." It's hard for me to believe that when the idea is formed, it comes with clarity about the level of importance and reach it could have. Entrepreneurs make 20-30 decisions a week, test over 1,000 ideas throughout their careers, and I think besides talent, we also seek a bit of the law of probabilities in the number of attempts we make, without neglecting learning. For me, that decision was to implement an efficient system that could produce on the line within a kitchen, to deliver food to the customer quickly, hot, and "freshly made." But I think the idea only came with the intention of being able to meet the demand of that small restaurant and thus make more money; the rest was operations management. They say the hamburgers from 1941 were a delight, there was nothing comparable, and the quality surpassed that of any other competitor, but do they still taste the same? Here we must ask ourselves, did their taste lead them to fleeting success, or was the concept what turned them into a multibillion-dollar business?

2. Chain Expansion:

The expansion of McDaniels is an epic tale of ambition and well-executed strategy. Imagine the visionaries behind McDaniels, contemplating a map and tracing the future territories of their empire. This was not a casual process but a series of calculated decisions. When McDaniels decided to expand, it was not simply about opening more locations but replicating their success formula in different markets. Each new McDaniels opening represented a unique challenge. The key was standardization and rigorous staff training, ensuring that every customer, no matter where in the world they were, received the same quality and experience. This uniformity created unwavering trust in the brand. The first locations outside their comfort zone proved that their model was scalable. The real achievement was maintaining the essence of the business while multiplying globally. The founders of McDaniels knew it was not just about selling hamburgers; it was about exporting an experience. The restaurants became ambassadors of their corporate culture and temples of operational consistency. This approach not only allowed rapid expansion but also cemented their reputation as a reliable and beloved brand, regardless of location. The expansion of McDaniels was more than a territorial conquest; it was building a global presence based on trust and quality.

3. Fierce Competition:

Fierce competition is a reality in any industry, and McDaniels has had its share of battles. Faced with rivals seeking to take their market share, McDaniels' strategy was always to stay one step ahead. It was not just about defending their position but constantly innovating to stay relevant and attractive. In the early days, when other players began to imitate their business model, McDaniels responded with agility and creativity. They improved their processes, introduced new products, and ensured their marketing was more effective than ever. For McDaniels, competition was not an obstacle but an opportunity to perfect themselves. Every competitor's move was meticulously analyzed, and every weakness turned into an area for improvement. Competitors could lower prices, but McDaniels chose not to engage in a destructive price war. They focused on adding value: from improving ingredient quality to offering faster and friendlier service. Competition pushed McDaniels to be more innovative, efficient, and customer-centric. Thus, the company not only survived but thrived in a fiercely competitive market.

4. Development of Combos:

The development of combos is one of those moments of brilliance that changes the game. For McDaniels, creating combos was not just a strategy to increase sales but a way to offer more value to their customers. I remember reading about how the founders realized they could simplify customer choice and simultaneously increase the average ticket by offering complete meals at a slightly reduced price. This approach made the customer experience more convenient and attractive. By packaging hamburgers, fries, and drinks, McDaniels not only facilitated purchase decisions but also increased operational efficiency. Kitchens could better predict demand and optimize production processes, reducing wait times and improving customer satisfaction. Combos became an integral part of McDaniels' identity. They also allowed easy introduction of new promotions and products. A new type of hamburger, for example, could be launched as part of a special combo, generating excitement and curiosity among customers. This approach also facilitated marketing strategies, allowing clearer and more effective communication of their offers.

5. **Adapting to Market Demand:**

Adapting to market demand is crucial for any business, and McDaniels has demonstrated exceptional skill in this aspect. The ability to read trends and respond quickly has been a key factor in their continued success. McDaniels not only listened to their customers but also anticipated their needs. In their early years, McDaniels realized that consumer tastes and preferences could vary greatly from one region to another. Thus, they began to adapt their menu to reflect local preferences. This approach allowed McDaniels to connect more deeply with their customers and stand out from their competitors. It was not just about offering fast food but the fast food that customers wanted at that specific time and place. Besides menu adaptations, McDaniels has also been agile in adjusting their marketing and operations strategies. During economic downturns, they introduced more economical options to attract budget-conscious customers. In times of heightened health awareness, they added healthier options to the menu. This flexibility and responsiveness have been essential to remaining relevant and competitive in a constantly changing market.

6. Prime Location Search:

Location is everything in the business world, and McDaniels understood this from the beginning. The strategy of seeking prime locations has been one of the pillars of their success. It was not simply about opening a restaurant anywhere available but identifying strategic points where they could maximize customer traffic. Think of high-traffic areas, near shopping centers, transportation hubs, and densely populated urban areas. McDaniels made an art of studying people's flow and selecting locations that guaranteed high visibility and accessibility. This strategy not only attracted more customers but also established McDaniels as a constant and reliable presence in people's daily lives. The location selection process involved meticulous analysis of demographic data, traffic patterns, and local competition. Each new opening was a calculated move, designed to capture the largest possible market. This attention to detail and ability to choose the best locations were fundamental to their expansion and sustained success. By always being in the right places, McDaniels ensured they were always on the consumer's mind, becoming a natural choice for a quick and delicious meal.

7. **Resistance to Price Wars:**

Resistance to price wars is a strategy that requires a lot of courage and vision. In a market where competition often lowers prices to attract customers, McDaniels took a different stance. Instead of participating in a race to the bottom, they decided to keep their prices stable and focus on added value. This approach demonstrated that McDaniels trusted the quality of their products and their customers' loyalty. They knew that competing solely on price could damage their brand perception and reduce long-term profitability. Instead, they focused on continuously improving the customer experience. By resistance, I mean they endured and then innovated, seeking ways not to always depend on price.

8. **Tenacity to Stay in the Created Market:**

Tenacity is an essential quality in any success story, and McDaniels has shown it in abundance. From their beginnings, they faced countless challenges, from fierce competition to market fluctuations. However, their determination to stay in the market they helped create never wavered. For McDaniels, staying in the market was not just about surviving but leading. This involved constant vigilance over emerging trends, a willingness to adapt, and a relentless pursuit of operational excellence. McDaniels' tenacity was reflected in their commitment to quality and innovation. They did not settle for initial success; they always sought ways to improve and offer more to their customers. McDaniels' corporate culture, based on perseverance and continuous improvement, was a key factor. They fostered an environment where resilience and the spirit of overcoming were valued. This mindset not only allowed them to overcome immediate challenges but also prepared them to face future obstacles with confidence and determination. McDaniels' tenacity is a powerful lesson on how persistence and adaptation can turn a company into a lasting leader in its industry.

9. Maximizing Profitability:

Maximizing profitability is both an art and a science, and McDaniels has perfected it over the years. Every aspect of their operation is designed to optimize profit margins, from ingredient acquisition to operational efficiency in restaurants. For McDaniels, profitability is not just about cutting costs but also increasing perceived value for the customer. One of the keys to their success has been implementing advanced management systems that allow rigorous cost control and resource maximization. Process standardization and continuous staff training ensure that each restaurant operates efficiently, minimizing waste and maximizing productivity. Additionally, McDaniels has successfully diversified their offerings with high-margin products like beverages and desserts, complementing their main sales. The combo strategy, previously mentioned, also played a crucial role in increasing profitability. By offering complete meals at a slightly reduced price, they managed to increase the average ticket and boost sales volume. Marketing strategies focused on promotions and upselling contributed to making each customer spend more with each visit. Lastly, leveraging technology and data analysis has allowed McDaniels to make informed and precise decisions to further optimize their operations and maintain a sustainable profit margin over time. This relentless focus on profitability has been a crucial component of their long-term success.

10. Marketing Vision:

Marketing vision is one of McDaniels' great strengths. From their early years, they understood the importance of creating a strong and recognizable brand. Effective marketing is not just about advertising but about creating an emotional connection with customers. McDaniels' marketing vision has been fundamental in establishing their presence and maintaining customer loyalty. They knew how to use storytelling and brand identity to create a powerful narrative. Every advertisement, slogan, and marketing campaign was carefully designed to reinforce McDaniels' values and promise. The marketing vision also involved leveraging technology and social media to stay relevant and connected with their audience. McDaniels embraced digital transformation early on, using data and analytics to understand their customers and personalize their marketing efforts. This approach allowed them to create highly effective campaigns and strengthen their brand presence in a constantly evolving market. The ability to tell their story, communicate their values, and adapt to changing trends has been key to their continued success. McDaniels' marketing vision is a powerful example of how a strategic and innovative approach can turn a brand into an icon in its industry.

With this final part, we conclude the story of a visionary brand that transcended its time, with pioneering and relentless leaders who turned their dream into a global empire. This story reminds us that success is not accidental but the result of vision, hard work, and the ability to adapt and innovate in a constantly changing world.

The 10 Steps to Apply This Strategy in Any Industry or Business:

1. Identify Complementary Products

The key to maximizing profitability doesn't always lie in the main product but in complementary products that can generate higher profit margins. Identifying these products requires a deep understanding of customer behavior and needs. For McDaniels, while burgers are the main product, fries, drinks, and desserts contribute significantly to their profits.

To apply this strategy to your business, start by analyzing what additional products or services could complement your main offering. These products should have a logical and appealing relationship with your main product. For example, if you have a bookstore, bookmarks, notebooks, and personalized coffee mugs can be ideal complementary products.

The next step is to analyze the profit margins of these products. Complementary products should have relatively low production costs but offer high perceived value to customers. This balance is crucial to ensure these products not only complement your main offering but also contribute significantly to your profitability.

Don't underestimate the power of market research in this process. Conduct surveys and interviews with your customers to better understand what other products they might be interested in buying along with your main offering. Use this information to adjust your inventory and offer products that not only increase sales but also enhance the overall customer experience.

2. Create Attractive Combos

Designing bundled packages or "combos" is an effective strategy to increase profitability by selling multiple products together at an attractive price. Combos not only increase the perceived value to the customer but also help move more inventory and increase the average purchase ticket.

To create attractive combos, start by identifying products that complement each other and together offer additional value to the customer. At McDaniels, a typical combo might include a burger, a portion of fries, and a drink, which provides a complete meal at a slightly lower price than if the products were purchased separately.

Designing these packages requires a well-thought-out pricing strategy. The goal is to offer a noticeable discount, but not so large that it significantly erodes profit margins. For example, if the sum of the individual prices of the products is $15, you could offer the combo at $13, so customers perceive a saving, but you still get a good profit margin.

Additionally, use presentation to make combos even more appealing. Use tempting images and attractive descriptions in your marketing materials to highlight the benefits of the combo. You might also consider creating themed or limited-time combos to generate urgency and attract more customers.

3. Establish Strategic Pricing

Strategic pricing is crucial to maximize profitability without alienating customers. Prices must be high enough to generate profits but also competitive and fair compared to market offerings.

First, conduct a detailed cost analysis to understand how much it costs to produce each product and combo. Include all direct and indirect costs, from raw materials to operating expenses. Once you have a clear understanding of your costs, set prices that ensure a healthy profit margin. Al

so, consider the perceived value of your products. Customers are willing to pay more for products they perceive as high quality or that offer significant added value. For example, a McDaniels combo might be perceived as good value because it offers a complete and convenient meal.

Implement different pricing strategies to maximize profitability. Psychological pricing, such as $9.99 instead of $10.00, can influence customer perception and make prices seem more attractive. You can also use price discrimination, offering different versions of a product at different prices to attract different customer segments.

Finally, regularly review and adjust your prices. The market changes, and it's crucial to adapt to new economic conditions, competition, and consumption trends. Use analytical tools to monitor the performance of your prices and make adjustments that maximize both sales and profit margins.

4. Implement Efficient Systems

Operational efficiency is key to reducing costs and improving profitability. Implementing efficient systems in the production and delivery of products can make a significant difference in overall business profitability.

For McDaniels, the development of an efficient kitchen system was a decisive factor in their success.

Start by analyzing your current processes and looking for areas of improvement. This might involve reorganizing the workspace to minimize unnecessary movements, automating repetitive tasks, or implementing new technologies to improve efficiency. A classic example is arranging the kitchen into specific stations for each task, minimizing the time and effort needed to prepare each order. Involve your team in this process.

Often, frontline employees have valuable ideas on how to improve efficiency. Foster a culture of continuous improvement where their suggestions are valued and implemented.

Additionally, invest in training to ensure all employees understand and follow the most efficient procedures. Regular training and skill development not only improve operational efficiency but also boost team morale and commitment.

Finally, use technological tools to monitor and optimize processes. Advanced point-of-sale systems, for example, can provide real-time data on sales and inventory, helping you make informed decisions and adjust processes accordingly. Technology can be a powerful ally in the quest for operational efficiency.

5. Invest in Technology

Technology is a crucial enabler for improving efficiency and gathering valuable customer data. Investing in the right technology can transform your operations and provide a significant competitive advantage. In the case of McDaniels, adopting advanced point-of-sale systems and mobile apps has been fundamental to optimizing their operations and enhancing the customer experience.

Start by assessing your current and future technological needs. Identify areas where technology can have the greatest impact, whether in inventory management, production efficiency, customer experience, or data collection. For example, a modern point-of-sale system not only speeds up the payment process but also provides valuable data on sales and customer behavior.

Adopting mobile apps can significantly enhance the customer experience. Offering the ability to place orders through a mobile app can increase convenience for customers and reduce wait times. Additionally, mobile apps can be a powerful tool for customer loyalty, allowing personalized promotions and reward programs.

Don't forget the importance of cybersecurity. As you integrate more technology into your operations, ensure you protect your customers' and your business's data against potential threats. Invest in adequate cybersecurity solutions and keep your systems updated.

Finally, use technology to collect and analyze data. Data can provide valuable insights into customer behavior, sales trends, and operational efficiency. Use this information to make informed decisions and adjust your strategy as needed.

6. Improve Customer Experience

Customer experience is a critical factor for the long-term success of any business. Improving the customer experience not only increases satisfaction and loyalty but can also boost sales and profitability. McDaniels has achieved this through constant renovations, additional services, and loyalty programs.

To improve the customer experience, start by evaluating the physical environment of your business. Make renovations or improvements to create a pleasant and welcoming atmosphere. This might include updated decor, comfortable seating, better lighting, and creating spaces that encourage social interaction.

Offer additional services that enhance customer convenience and satisfaction. This might include self-service options, mobile device charging stations, or free Wi-Fi availability. Think about how you can make a customer's visit more comfortable and enjoyable.

Develop loyalty programs that reward frequent customers. Points programs, exclusive discounts, and personalized promotions can incentivize customers to return. Use technology to manage these programs and personalize rewards based on each customer's purchase behavior.

Finally, train your staff to provide exceptional customer service. Friendliness, efficiency, and problem-solving skills are essential qualities for any customer service team. Invest in ongoing training and set clear service standards to ensure every customer has a positive experience in every interaction with your business.

7. **Diversify the Menu (Catalog and Offer)**

Diversifying your offer is essential to remain relevant and attract new market segments. For McDaniels, including healthier options and alternatives has been key to adapting to changing consumer demands.

Introduce new products strategically, starting with pilot tests before a full implementation. This will allow you to evaluate market acceptance and adjust the offer as necessary. Use promotions and special events to generate interest and attract customers to try new options.

Don't forget to maintain a balance between innovation and consistency. While diversifying your menu, ensure that new products meet the same quality standards as your main offerings. Diversification should not compromise your brand's reputation or customer satisfaction.

8. **Constantly Analyze and Adjust**

Continuous tracking and adjustment are crucial for the long-term success of any business strategy. Regularly monitor sales, profit margins, and customer satisfaction to identify areas for improvement and make necessary adjustments.

Use analytical tools to collect and analyze data. Point-of-sale systems and business management applications can provide detailed information on product performance and operational efficiency. Analyze this data to identify patterns and trends that can inform your decisions.

Establish key performance indicators (KPIs) to evaluate the success of your strategies. These metrics can include average revenue per customer, customer return rate, profit margin per product, and customer satisfaction. Use these metrics to measure progress and adjust your tactics as needed.

Implement a continuous feedback loop. Involve your employees and customers in the feedback process to gain valuable insights into what is working and what isn't. Use this feedback to make quick adjustments and continuously improve your operations and marketing strategies.

Finally, maintain a flexible and open mindset to change. The market and customer preferences are constantly evolving, and it is crucial to adapt to these changes to stay competitive. Being willing to adjust your approach based on data and feedback can help you optimize profitability and maintain a competitive edge.

9. **Adapt to the Market**

Adapting to market conditions and competitor actions is essential to maintaining relevance and long-term success. Stay aware of market trends, innovations, and competitor strategies to adjust your approach accordingly.

Conduct periodic market studies to identify changes in customer preferences and market conditions. Use this information to adapt your offer and marketing strategy.

Closely monitor your competitors. Analyze their strategies, products, and marketing tactics to identify opportunities and threats. Use this information to differentiate your offer and find your niche in the market.

Be proactive rather than reactive. Instead of waiting for market changes to affect you, look for opportunities to lead the change. Innovate and experiment with new ideas to stay ahead of the competition and meet your customers' evolving needs.

Finally, be flexible and ready to adjust your strategies quickly. Market conditions can change rapidly, and it is crucial to respond quickly to maintain competitiveness and profitability.

10.　　Focus on Long-Term Profitability

Prioritizing sustainable long-term profitability is fundamental for ongoing success. While it may be tempting to seek quick gains, long-term strategies that invest in growth and continuous improvement tend to be more effective.

Start by setting clear and realistic long-term financial goals. These goals should include not only revenue and profits but also investments in infrastructure, technology, and training. Develop a financial plan that balances short-term gains with the necessary investments for future growth.

Invest in quality and innovation. Customer satisfaction and brand loyalty are essential for long-term profitability. Ensure that your products and services maintain high quality standards and continue to innovate to keep your offerings relevant and attractive.

Develop strong relationships with your suppliers and business partners. These relationships can provide stability and opportunities to improve efficiency and reduce costs in the long run. Negotiate favorable contracts and seek strategic alliances that benefit both parties.

Finally, maintain a focus on sustainability. Social and environmental responsibility is increasingly important to consumers and can be a key differentiator. Implement sustainable practices in your business that not only benefit the environment but also enhance your reputation and attract more conscious customers.

By following these steps, any business can apply the strategy of complementary products to maximize profitability. These principles can be adapted and implemented in any industry to achieve significant results.

Quick Guide: Profitability Strategy with Complementary Products

1. Identify complementary products:

Find products or services that complement your core offering and have high profit margins.

2. Create attractive bundles:

Design combined packages that offer additional value to the customer and increase profitability.

3. Establish strategic pricing:

Set prices that maximize profitability while remaining attractive to customers.

4. Implement efficient systems:

Optimize processes and systems to reduce costs and waiting times.

5. Invest in technology:

Use technological tools to improve efficiency and gather valuable data.

6. Enhance customer experience:

Seek ways to improve customer experience through renovations, additional services, and loyalty programs.

7. Diversify the menu:

Introduce new and relevant options to meet changing market demands.

8. Constantly analyze and adjust:

Regularly track sales and customer satisfaction to make necessary adjustments.

9. Adapt to the market:

Stay informed about market trends and competitors' actions to adjust your strategy.

10. Focus on long-term profitability:

Prioritize strategies that ensure sustainable long-term profitability.

Conclusion

Upon reflecting on the depth of analysis and the richness of examples explored in this guide, it becomes evident that the strategy of driving profitability through complementary products and attractive combinations is not just a business tactic, but an art in itself. From the humble beginnings of McDaniel's to the global expansion of OK.EA, we have navigated through a variety of industries and companies to understand how this strategy has been successfully implemented time and again.

At every step along the way, patterns and lessons emerge that transcend industry boundaries and markets. The need to identify opportunities within the existing portfolio, the importance of constant innovation, meticulous attention to customer experience, and agility to adapt to changing market demands are fundamental elements resonating throughout each success story.

In a world where competition is fierce and customer expectations are constantly evolving, the ability to think creatively and strategically is more valuable than ever. This guide has provided a deep insight into how businesses can leverage complementary products, bundled packages, and strategic pricing to drive profitability and remain relevant in an ever-changing business environment.

Ultimately, what becomes clear is that business excellence is not merely the result of a single brilliant strategy, but rather the outcome of a series of smart, adaptive decisions made with a profound understanding of the market, customers, and the company's own strengths and weaknesses. With a commitment to continuous improvement and the ability to learn from both successes and failures of the past, any company can chart its own path towards sustainable profitability and long-term growth.